" Steven Ing's teachings have much to offer our society concerning a discussion around sexuality. His down-to-earth tone provides the reader with a comfortable, wise and practical way to discuss sexual matters without fear of embarrassment or shame."

Dr. Tory Clark

• **D.H.S., M.P.H., L.A.D.C-I**

" Sex, like death, is an experience that connects us all with its invisible tendons, but still it separates us with a pervasive silence. Our silence. We sing about love but flatly refuse to talk about sex – which can make us victims to its powers and provocations. Steven Ing is no victim. And his open, honest book can help parents and partners alike break the silence surrounding this most human and nurturing experience. Yes, there is something quite beautiful and liberating in these pages."

Damian Geddry

• **M.A.R., Claremont School of Theology • Chair, Hagen Place • Co-Chair, The Gooden Center**

sexual futurist .com illuminating the world through reason and knowledge.

we're all like this | **STEVEN ING, M.A., M.F.T.**

we're all like this | **STEVEN ING, M.A., M.F.T.**

photography | **CHRIS HOLLOMAN**

First Giant Publishing Edition July 2015

Published in the United States of America by Giant Publishing, Tucson, Arizona.

Library of Congress Control Number: 2015944059

ISBN-10: 1-933975-07-5
ISBN-13: 978-1-933975-07-8

10 9 8 7 6 5 4 3 2

All images used by permission.
WWW.SEXUALFUTURIST.COM

WWW.GIANTPUBLISHING.COM

GIANT PUBLISHING

table of CONTENTS

Of all the dimensions of the human experience only one receives sustained pressure to remain outside the realm of normal conversation, resting undisclosed and unknown. Ordinary human sexual needs are the one kind of human need our species just hasn't learned how to talk about. Contrary to what some might think, avoiding talking about our sexuality is not limited to cultures influenced by Puritans, the Taliban or other religious groups who are frequently held responsible for our silence. Routinely in many cultures around the world one sees an inability to talk about real human sexual needs. Virtually no one is teaching us to talk about our sexual needs in a manner that is empowering, helpful or perhaps even uplifting or enlightening.

In contrast, consider how comfortably we explore, study and accept our neediness in other dimensions of the human experience. When we consider physical needs, virtually any schoolchild can rattle off, "food, water, clothing, and shelter." With more education, we come to understand that our physical needs for food include a certain caloric intake required to maintain our metabolism; protein, fats and carbohydrates in a proper balance; vitamins and minerals in recommended daily amounts and so forth. The media seems to (daily!) publish results from new studies adding to our knowledge of nutrition and other physical needs like our minimum requirements for sleep, light exposure and clean air free of contaminants like cigarette smoke. In all of these discussions of human needs we typically define "need" as "that which is required for the organism to survive." This book, in contrast, looks differently at the word "need." In this book we will be using the word "need" to mean "that which the organism requires, not to survive, but to thrive."

Take but a moment to consider how we usually talk about our needs. Usually, whether we mean to survive or to thrive, we're quite comfortable and articulate. In fact, of the many dimensions of the human experience such as intellect, feelings, or social lives--each comes with its own set of needs. Most dimensions of the human experience receive the same passionate scrutiny, study, and dissemination as, say, our need for food. We argue about how much of this or how little of that we should be eating.

Likewise, we debate children's intellectual needs in the form of arguments about curriculum, methods of teaching, and length of education requirements. We comfortably accept the notion that, like our nutritional needs, our intellectual needs continue throughout the lifespan and include adults' needs for intellectual stimulation, gratification, growth and expression.

We accept that all humans have emotional needs. What kind of monstrous parents would claim that a children does not need love, comfort or joy. No parent worthy of the name would deny that our children have a human right to feelings and to learn how to incorporate their knowledge of how they feel into the formulation of their decisions. No one doubts that these emotional needs continue beyond our childhood years or that they extend right up to the final breath we take upon our deathbeds.

Only a child with monsters or morons for parents would be left without any provision to address his social needs. What parent seeing his child without a friend in the world would not feel broken-hearted over such a state? We intuitively know, and would be less than human if we didn't, that our children (and by extension, all children) need companionship, social intercourse and the stimulation of sharing time and thoughts with others. We understand that these needs only dim with the passing of life.

Even those of us who are most irreligious would loathe to claim that our children, even atheist children, have no spiritual needs. All humans have a spiritual viewpoint over how the unseen bits of this universe exist and what they mean to us and our fellows—even atheists. Certainly parents and others differ about what our spiritual needs are—we might well argue for example whether our children should be enrolled in formal religious training, or simply left alone. Some might even suggest we would perhaps be best taught to appreciate Nature and the meaning it brings to the human experience. But there is no argument that human beings have spiritual needs to know why we're here, to have some understanding of our place in the universe and to come to some inner peace about those aspects of the human experience that cry out for meaning and for understanding.

In the same manner we have financial needs and we know about (and argue about) our financial needs for resources, training and mentoring—but there is no argument about having such needs. We universally agree that people have recreational needs to have fun and we agree that these needs begin in childhood and endure throughout the lifespan; children have playgrounds and grown-ups take vacations and both have hobbies and pastimes because of this universal understanding of the need for play and recreation.

Our aesthetic needs for beauty in our lives is also understood, accepted and easily discussed. We collect art, we publicly fund museums and other public art displays or sometimes we even just paint a wall in our homes because of our aesthetic need for beauty in our lives. No one suggests we might seriously make our way through life more prudently by seeking out physically unattractive mates, cultivate facial or other bodily distortions or buy only homes utterly lacking in charm. No one wishes to listen to music they find distasteful; quite the contrary, we need to listen to beautiful music. We gravitate to beauty as matter gravitates to mass, only rather than a law of nature, this attraction to beauty is a law of our nature.

But something happens when we need to talk about our sexual needs. In the discussion of human sexuality there is a sort of blindness. This blindness results in the absence of any intelligent discussion (or any intelligent management!) of our sexual needs. The vast majority of contemporary public conversations about sexuality is left to one of two extremes—either the religious fundamentalists or political extremists with an overly simplified system of "Thou shalt not!" or the vulgar rants of radio shock jocks and the like. Neither of these two extremes presents a thoughtful, considered discussion of the notion of our collective and individual sexual needs. Similarly, parents and their children, lovers (or would be lovers) and even spouses are generally unable to intelligently hold even one of the thousands of needed conversations about this extremely important matter.

In my work as a counselor I have had the privilege of interviewing thousands of individuals and couples about sexual matters. Routinely I have asked them whether they and their spouse or lover could talk comfortably about sex. All of them have said, "Yes, of course." Upon further questioning, a very different story unfolds. This story reveals that, even in their most private conversations with their most intimate of associates, most of us are unable to discuss their sexual thoughts, feelings, behaviors, fantasies or histories. What they mean when they say they can talk about sex is that they can use the word "sex" in a sentence—so long as it isn't too personal: "How about doing it tonight?"

Our inability to talk clearly about sexuality is a reflection of our inability to think about it clearly. This book is an attempt to provide the language that would allow all of us to begin discussing sexual matters in a simple and human way. Without such a model, even the religious who think they should be the ones to talk to their children about sex, simply wouldn't know how to do so. Without such a model, even the nonreligious who think they and their children will be free of the rotting influence of religion will only find themselves without any meaningful language. If only they had the words, lovers could really enjoy each other more instead of just hoping things would work out. Spouses could tell one another about their changing needs as their years together speed by all too quickly.

In the last century, therapists who worked with alcoholics and listened to their stories learned about dysfunctional families. Through watching and listening to so many similar stories they eventually figured out how normal families should work. In this way then, alcoholics and their families gave the gift of a new understanding in the field of family therapy.

In the same way my work with sex offenders has taught me about their sexually dysfunctional history. Sex offenders tend to have awful sex lives—awfully boring and awfully unfulfilling. Their sex lives are sometimes nonexistent except for the crime that got them in trouble! Most of them seem far more pathetic than predatory. Therapy that empowers them to lawfully and honorably get their needs met is vastly more effective than the more commonly used techniques of repression, that is, teaching them to even further distance themselves from their sexual needs. Teaching them how to powerfully and joyfully embrace their sexuality and sexual needs has helped me understand what normal humans need in the same way that understanding alcoholic families helped all of us learn how to be healthier.

I expect to hear from some who differ with my conclusions. There will doubtless be those who simply deny that people have sexual needs or who deny that those needs are as I have outlined them in this book. But whenever one attempts to codify any information helpful to the race of humanity as a whole there is invariably an outcry regarding exceptions or that what is mainly true, overwhelming true is somehow of little value to humanity because there is some exception…somewhere. "I knew someone who didn't need sex at all," for example. But general truths, nearly universal truths, are still rather important.

Some will differ about the exact nature of our sexual needs and still others will deny that we have sexual needs at all. How will preachers in the future hector congregants about their sexual sins when the people in the pews simply want guidance about how to get their legitimate sexual needs met. If all of us have sexual needs and the needs are, in fact, needs--then what of the prohibition on the sort of "cruel and unusual punishment" that locks men away for decades inside sterile boxes. One can only imagine the impact on public policy for children, teenagers, seniors in assisted living and those miserable souls who have no right whatsoever to feel as miserable as they do in relationships that are not meeting their needs.

Our sexual needs are constantly present, yet always changing. They are lifelong, yet developmental; idiosyncratic, yet universally shared. It is a moral principle of humanity that the individual is the only one who can rightfully determine which of his needs he will ignore. Thus, I might forego a meal (or many meals) and that is certainly my right. But it is wrong of others to deprive me of my right to eat.

Some will complain of this book's lack of scientific rigor in talking about what is the most human, most intimate part of who we are. Perhaps we don't need more experiments; perhaps we just need to think about who we really are.

My body tells me what I need. Using what are usually called "thought experiments" we can ask ourselves to imagine having the perfect life, the perfect life partner—and then we can consider eliminating one aspect of that perfect life—sexual play and humor for example. Would the "perfect life" or the "perfect sex life" be perfect anymore if everything were as serious as a heart attack? Would such a life even be sustainable? Not for most of us. The book you are holding will equip you to talk about these sexual needs in a real and genuine way that will guard your dignity. You will begin to know and understand yourself in a way that will allow you to let other people get to know you as much as you like. You will experience a deeper spirituality as the most intimate parts of your body and the most personal longings of your heart become seen as blessings rather than trials. This book is designed to help you and your family learn how to talk comfortably about sex. The book is designed to be the sort of book that, set out on a coffee table, might be picked up by anyone under your roof (family member or guest, young or old) without fear of embarrassment. Children, parents, and lovers alike will likely find the book helpful in learning how to talk about the many aspects of this important part of what it means to be human.

My fondest hope is that we will not need to learn from our own errors exclusively; that we could learn from the very painful lessons of those whose ignorance of their sexual needs led them to hurt themselves and others—sometimes beyond words. Even those who read these pages will make mistakes but with a father's heart I wish for all of you that your mistakes too will become part of a beautiful learning experience of how to intelligently manage your human sexuality.

This book grew mostly out my work. I have been a marriage and family counselor for decades now but in recent years I have worked mostly with men and women who've committed sexual crimes. In the rewarding and deeply satisfying work with them, certain patterns made themselves known through sheer repetition. It may strike some as an unexpected revelation (I know it did me) that sex offenders mostly commit their crimes not out of a sense of strength and mastery or any real sense of power; rather, they commit their crimes out of a sense of disempowerment. They only seem predatory because they so often are seeking a person or situation where they feel some sense of empowerment. They are pretenders to the style of the powerful; they are not truly powerful. Typically, even if married or with a partner, they are not happy. If they have high paying jobs, they are not satisfied or fulfilled. Their careers are not truly meaningful and satisfying to them. They do not have close friends who truly know them and love them. They do not have good love lives. Their relationships are not working the way they should. They are more pathetic than they are predatory.

The sex lives of those who commit sex crimes are, at the time of their offense, invariably boring and unsatisfying on so many levels. Many do not even have sex lives; some 5 percent of the men with whom I have worked are virgins; hardly the stereotype--virgin sex offenders! Many of those who've never been with a partner sexually have never even dated, they've never asked a woman out, and they've never initiated so much as even an intimate conversation with a partner. Most of those who have engaged in sex or who have dated or who have had conversations with potential mates have done these things at such a poor level of intimacy that only one conclusion is possible: they do not know what they are doing. And that is the reason I wrote this book—too many people don't know about healthy intimacy because we seem willing to let every generation figure it out on their own. The real reason we don't teach our children better is because so often we ourselves are still figuring it out.

I also counsel married couples who are not sex offenders and their problems were often similar to those noted in the offenders. The troubled people in these relationships are not acting in a criminal manner. Sometimes however they are acting out sexually—by using sex as a weapon to punish one another, as a reward to get something they want—or they are having affairs or in some other way violating the promises they made to their spouse. It seemed as though nearly everyone coming into my office was having sexual problems that were not addressed by standard counseling practice, medicines, or sex education.

Typical was their response to the question of whether they and their spouse or lover could talk comfortably about sex. Everyone would say, "Yes, of course." That they were self-deceived in this response became clear later in the interview. I would ask them sometime later in their appointment what they think about when they're having sex and they would answer forthrightly something to the effect that, "Oh, I think about her," or "I think about how good it feels." I would dutifully note their response and then offhandedly ask, "Oh, and what does your mate think about?" Invariably, the answer was something like, "Gee, I have no idea," or "I never asked." Later in the interview I would ask the client to briefly describe three of their typical sexual fantasies. Again, they were quite comfortable telling me, a relative stranger about this intimate part of their lives; but when I asked them to describe their mate's fantasies, invariably the response was the same as those above, "I have no idea," or "We never talked about that," or "I'm afraid what the answer might be." As the session went on I would ask about sexual histories and other very intimate matters. My clients were always willing to discuss these matters, but, when asked about their mate's past and so forth, the response was the same—they were unsure and uncomfortable. They would say, "We never talked about that," or "We try to leave the past in the past."

This pattern invariably occurred literally thousands of times. I am convinced that, although most couples in the world have sex, very few couples are able to talk about having sex. In these most intimate and important of relationships, often between individuals who've known each other for years, very few of them actually know one another. They "do it," but they cannot talk about doing it.

Yet they think they can. After starting off, "Oh yeah, sure, we can talk about sex," some people finish the interview and then realize something is wrong. I might comment, "So when you said you two could talk about sex I guess you didn't mean your sexual thoughts, your sexual feelings, your sexual histories or your sexual behavior." Their response was sometimes, "Gee, I guess we really don't talk sex." Mostly they didn't even notice during our session, except to realize that they certainly were uncomfortable during the discussion. One time a man looked surprised and then clarified, "When I said we could talk about sex I meant we could ask each other, 'Do you want to do it?' That's as much as we talked about it."

My clients with criminal histories showed me their patterns over time; what surprised me was that all of my clients, both those with and those without a criminal history were essentially the same. They were the same in their inability to talk comfortably, intimately and rationally about sex with their mates or people of interest. The difference was that my noncriminal clients had more highly evolved relational and social skills that allowed them either to get their needs met within the law—or to obtain enough diversion to minimize the personal impact of their intimacy deficits.

This book attempts to provide the language that would allow all of us to begin discussing sexual matters in a manner that is straightforward (unlike some religious fundamentalists) and offers human dignity in the process (unlike many others). Without such a model, even the religious, who think they should be the ones to talk to their children about sex, simply cannot do so because they don't know how. Without such a model, the vulgar individual simply trying to draw attention to himself wouldn't know how to actually have an intimate conversation.

Initially, we may be tempted to blame Christian forbears for the shame and incompetence in discussing and managing such an innately integral part of our human experience. "Oh, those Puritans," some might be tempted to say. But then there is the Taliban and others in the community of Islam who are also terribly uncomfortable with such matters. We might say, "Well, it's the religious people; apparently, God is not so great after all." But this conclusion, too, would be wrong because even atheists and subcultures largely influenced by atheism have the same difficulty in talking about sexual matters and teaching other people how to talk about sexual needs and sexual matters. The inability to comfortably communicate about sexuality is a global problem that is surely an indicator of the next needed step in our species' social evolution. There is no one to blame and no solution to the problem to be found in blaming. The problem of a pathological level of prudery is universal. Our failure as a species to intelligently grapple with this problem has left the subject to the mangling of those who would use sex to control others—or to those at the other extreme of prudery—the glib libertine. Both the prude and the libertine exploit human sexuality for their own short-term purposes.

In the three years since this book was first written I began posting blogs on the website called Sexual Futurist. Now there are many sexual futurists who use reason and knowledge to begin conversations about human sexuality. We have created a sexual Bill of Rights for everyone and everyone is invited to weigh in as we continue a conversation about human sexuality. Thousands of us take part in this conversation. We are a diverse group sexually and in every other way—but like all of humanity we are all far more alike than we are different.

I initially thought of this book as an aid to sex offenders in their recoveries. I was confident it could help them. Then I began to see how it could help prevent sex crimes if only I could get it into the hands (and heads) of young people so that they could begin solving their sexual problems like people solve other problems—by talking about them and managing their problems intelligently. I've come to realize that everyone needs to be able to talk about sexual needs with the same comfort level as when talking about needing anything else. I realized that this is a book for the single woman awash in her modernity, who deals with loneliness—even in her marriage. It is for the young father who takes his children to religious services and wants his children to have happy and fulfilling lives even as he remains in denial about his own life. This book is for children also since they too want to know how talk about this important part of life. Who wouldn't want their spouse, their children, and their society to be able to talk about sexuality in a rational, comfortable and helpful manner?

The goal in all this talking, talking, and more talking is nothing less than the promotion of clear thinking about sexuality which would result in healthier sexual choices for all of us. Our personal happiness and the success of human civilization depend on a rational discussion of sexual matters particularly in an age where ideology and emotional reactivity so often trump evidence and reason. To that end this work is dedicated.

Steven Ing, M.A., M.F.T.

WHILE WE WERE STILL VERY YOUNG

Our sexuality has been with us from birth. Between the time we were born and right up until we become physically sexually mature (a time referred to as "puberty"), a number of sexual needs make themselves known. All of these needs, remember, come under that heading of "that which is required, not to survive, but to thrive." Starting with the need for sexual safety and ending with the need for sexual dignity, all of these needs are clearly part of who we are long before we are physically sexually mature.

Our sexual needs run together inside of us. So, our need for sexual privacy is part of our need for sexual safety. Our need for sexual privacy begins in our earliest days and is part of our need to learn sexual boundaries. We need sexual privacy because sharing ultimately depends on letting others have access to what is mine.

We can talk about any human need with words and so we can discuss our need for sleep separately from our need to breathe—but in real life, in our own bodies these two needs clearly overlap one another. But we ourselves cannot be so easily and so neatly divided. Our sexual needs for safety, for play and for dignity and indeed, all of our sexual needs, run together, overlapping and supporting one another. This is just like any discussion of our humanity in that within each of us lie many parts, each with their own needs—but we are still one whole person. We're simple, really, but not that simple. We're complicated, but not so complicated we cannot understand ourselves. Understanding our sexuality is impossible unless we develop the language to explain our needs.

we're all like this | **STEVEN ING**

chapter 1 | SAFETY

The most universal sexual need shared by everyone is that of sexual safety. From the self-confident urban adult to the frail senior citizen to the infant born just moments ago—all of us have a need for our sexual dignity and physical integrity to be protected. Because of this fact then, we can say with confidence that everyone has sexual needs. When we were very young, the only sexual need we might really have had is exclusively that of sexual safety.

We don't argue that workers have a right to a safe workplace although we may differ about how to achieve that goal or what the phrase "a safe workplace" might mean. In the same way we believe schools, homes and medical care should all be safe. No one argues about this. And no one makes any sort of serious argument (especially to a loving parent!) that children don't have a need to be kept safe. Sexual safety is a part of simply being safe in a general way.

Can our need for sexual safety change over time? Some of our needs, including the specifics of ensuring our safety may evolve. Many adults spend a great deal of effort figuring out (and sometimes ignoring) their own need for safety—but the need is still there. Ignorance of a need doesn't mean we don't have such a need. Our needs for sexual safety include keeping ourselves and our children emotionally safe from overwhelming experiences that would endanger our physical, mental and emotional health. Just as adults evolve over time and their needs for safety change so too with children as they change over their years in the home.

Children need to grow up without anyone violating their sexual integrity. All touches should be safe. All discussions should be respectful—which is not to say they cannot be lighthearted. Children need to be understood in light of their needs for healthy sexual development. This means that ignoring a child's sexual development is wrong. We ignore no other aspect of a child's development. Why, other than simple ignorance, would we ignore this part of a child's upbringing? The need for safety is going to include age-appropriate instruction on how to stay safe as one gets older.

The need for sexual safety begins at birth and it never goes away. Not knowing about your need for safety as a child doesn't mean you don't have such a need. The need for safety may not be known to a baby, but nevertheless the baby needs to be kept safe sexually. Your own need for sexual safety may not be fully known or understood by you, but rest assured you are normal in your need to be and feel safe when dealing with sexual matters. This safe feeling will give you the power to explore your sexuality and understand this powerful natural force. Although your needs for sexual safety will change and develop over time this need will never go away. Our recognition and acceptance of this need will help us to live our lives intelligently and successfully.

we're all like this | **STEVEN ING**

chapter 2 | INNOCENCE

Innocence is the freedom from knowledge of matters we are too immature to process in a healthy manner. We protect young people from knowledge of this sort so that they may be allowed to mature gracefully and with strength as some knowledge is simply too much for them. Because of this concern for children's need for innocence we protect them from adult financial worries and from violence that is real but considered injurious to young minds. In a similar way we sometimes protect the young from sexual information and experiences that may otherwise be true or even good—but are too much for them.

Some sexual information and experiences are too much for younger people because they do not have the life experience to put such information into perspective or to comprehend the meanings of certain experiences. Sometimes the young simply cannot make good judgments about things like money, weapons, politics and sexual matters because they haven't yet learned enough about related matters that color meanings and direct decision-making. When discussing sexual matters children have the right to the information that will protect them. But safety of the body is not the only protection children need. Young people need protection of their childhood experience. They need protection of their imaginations.

Formal sex education programs through the public school system often push all children through the same education at the same time in the same way. This is not likely to be the best approach to care for children as such an approach does not allow children to develop in different manners and at different rates. Just as their bodies and their sexuality develop at different rates, so too do their minds. But this is not the worst liability of many mass sex education programs.

Public sex education programs tend to focus, quite understandably since they are funded by the state, on prevention of unwanted pregnancy, methods of birth control and prevention of disease. These are important concerns to any community. Yet as important as such information is, it is woefully inadequate in that such an approach is founded on a fear-based, mechanistic view of sex. There is nothing here to help children understand the wonder and joy of human sexuality. The wonder and joy our species finds in sharing love in this way is, at its best, full of meaning, full of beauty and full of spiritual importance. Teaching a child about reproduction, disease and pregnancy is only the tiniest part of sexuality. This reduction of human sexuality to disease and pregnancy prevention does children no favors in savaging their innocence. This way of thinking is not an argument against sexual education; it is an argument for making sexual educations more comprehensive and more human.

The need for sexual innocence begins at birth and it never goes away completely. Even the seasoned professional who deals with sexual matters of all sorts every workday needs to be able to let go of the adult concerns in these matters when he returns to his private life. Not knowing about your need for innocence doesn't mean there is no such need. We look at the baby and can see his own need in this matter even if baby cannot. Your own need for sexual innocence may not be fully known or understood by you but rest assured you are normal in your need to be and to feel innocent when dealing with sexual matters. This innocence will give you the power to explore the joy, the beauty and the spirituality of this powerful natural force. Although your needs for sexual innocence will change and develop over time this need will never go away.

we're all like this | **STEVEN ING**

chapter 3 | INFORMATION

All children need education on sexual matters, because sex and the vast world of human sexuality has the potential to bring great joy or great misery into our lives. To rear a child with deliberate or accidental avoidance of sexual matters is a great disservice to that child.

All too often sex education is reduced to a bare bones curriculum of lessons on sexual body parts, the way those parts work and how to prevent getting a disease or having an unwanted pregnancy. These lessons are not bad in themselves; but they alone are not nearly enough. We must include information that affirms the right to simply be a sexual being, which means identifying my needs and managing them appropriately as I become an adult. Our sexual education begins in infancy, the moment we are born and identified by gender. "It's a girl!" or "It's a boy!"

Immediately, we are relating to the world and the world is relating to us as sexual beings. As infants, we learn that the world is safe or dangerous for us to be sexual when we are taught to be happy or disapproving of our bodies. As young children, we become aware of the differences between the normal loving affection a parent gives a child and the different sort of hugs and kisses parents give each other. Awareness of this difference forms a critical part of our sexual education.

In addition to learning about our own bodies and how they work, all of us should be learning how wonderful, mysterious and powerful the world of sexuality is. We need to learn how unmet sexual needs can trick us into thinking something we otherwise wouldn't think if our needs were met. For example, some people marry the wrong person because they mistake sexual attraction for compatibility. For this reason we must also learn to talk comfortably about sexual matters with family, friends, professionals and prospective mates. The need to learn this way of thinking begins before we become sexually mature.

This process of learning continues throughout our lives. No one knows all there is to know about human sexuality. This is true because experience is essential to true knowledge of sexuality and some experiences depend on aging. We experience life developmentally. Our tastes in food change during our lives and certain foods we loved in our youth become distasteful to us later and vice versa. So too with sexuality, our tastes and desires change. Young children may be put off by the idea of physically expressing affection in the ways adults do in consensual adult relationships. Older people who once liked one way of expressing affection may grow to prefer other ways, disdaining their former tastes.

The need for reliable, accurate sexual information is always with us and this need never goes away. Everyone has this normal need and so do you, whether you are aware of it or not. You are normal in your need for sexual information. The need for helpful sexual information begins at birth. You will always have this need and, though this need will change over time, it will never go away.

We must be open-minded to learning because until we know, we cannot make intelligent decisions and guide our lives successfully. Your own need for sexual information may not be fully known or understood by you but rest assured you are normal in your need to know and no one has the right to withhold from you timely and relevant sexual information. The safe feeling you get from knowing what's going on will give you the ability to explore your sexuality safely and to understand this powerful natural force. Although your knowledge will grow over your lifetime, you will always be learning and the need for sexual information will never go away.

we're all like this | **STEVEN ING**

chapter 4 | BEING SEXUAL

To simply allow myself (and be allowed by others) to be a sexual being is challenging but always essential. Being sexual means we sometimes talk about sex, ask questions about sex, have sexual thoughts and frequently look at people and have sexual feelings of attraction. Merely being sexual is like allowing myself to experience some other part of my identity, such as my intellectual or emotional or even social self. How are people simply to be sexual without offending others or without violating the boundaries of others?

One good way is simply give oneself permission to have sexual thoughts and feelings without thinking there is a need to repress them. My thoughts and feelings are my own. No one has a need to feel offended by them. For example, if I find someone "very attractive," that simply means I am attracted to that person. This feeling is normal and mostly unremarkable because we normally find many people attractive in this world. This attraction is often mutual but even more often is not mutual. That too is alright, since mere attraction is an everyday event, a normal part of life.

Another way to simply be sexual is to enjoy the feelings of sexual health and the sense of vitality that comes with sexual health. To savor the vibrant feelings of desire, even unfulfilled desire, is to savor a vibrant color from life's palette. As we allow ourselves to simply exist as sexual beings, we begin to know our humble place as a part of the universe's cycle of life. Likewise, even though none of us may be attractive to all others, all of us are attractive to some. To enjoy this feeling of attractiveness and the power associated with it is neither evil nor harmful; enjoying this feeling is simply part of being a sexual being.

There are many who are frightened of sex and the power that flows out of individual sexuality. The fact that we cannot control who is attracted to us or the strength of our own feelings maddens some people who cannot accept their humanity. Often, such individuals try to control others through guilt, shame and even different forms of physical repression— like telling adults what clothing to wear. None of these efforts are effective in a larger sense. There can be no effective control—only well informed management of one's own sexuality. After we accept that we are sexual beings we can intelligently direct our sexuality in those ways that leave us feeling comfortable.

You are normal in your need to simply be who you are; the alternative is to try to be someone you are not, to be a fake version of yourself. You are normal in feeling your need to simply be sexual. The need to simply be the sexual beings we are begins at birth and it never goes away. Even the baby is watching as mom and dad kiss and hug—or when they fail to do so. And by watching, the baby is learning how to live and how to someday deal with this kissing and hugging business. Not knowing about your inescapable need to simply be a sexual being doesn't mean you don't have such a need. Accepting ourselves as sexual beings helps us to make intelligent decisions in situations where sexual feelings are a part of the issue at hand— like marriage. Accepting our sexual feelings helps us to consider intelligent alternatives in sexual matters. Your own need to simply be a sexual being may not be fully known or understood by you but rest assured you are normal in this. The relaxed feeling you get from simply being yourself in this sexual way will give you the ability to explore your sexuality safely and to better understand this powerful natural force. Although we begin life as babies and hopefully die at a much older age, throughout the whole of life we will be sexual beings.

we're all like this | STEVEN ING

chapter 5 | BOUNDARIES

Boundaries refers to the limits we need to feel safe and comfortable. Personal boundaries are like the boundaries between countries or between neighbors. They define the limits of our legitimate power. So long as I am on the right side of my limits of legitimate power and you are on yours then we can have peace between us.

We have moral boundaries for treating others that we must respect. We have other moral boundaries that apply to the way others treat us. When people cross over those boundaries we feel offended, angry and violated.

When we talk about sexual boundaries, we're talking about both the boundaries I have for myself (what I feel is right and proper for my behavior) and about what I feel is right and proper for you when you are interacting with me. Sometimes people get confused about boundaries and think that, because they are offended, a legitimate boundary was violated. We must be careful in our thinking here as we may not be defending our boundaries so much as simply trying to control others because we are afraid of what they are doing. For example, consider the case where someone we know is reading a sexual book or magazine that we find unacceptable for ourselves for some reason. Clearly, what one person is reading is of no concern whatsoever in terms of violating the boundaries of another person. Another example would be that found in the other, private moments of those people who may be doing something we would not approve of for ourselves—such matters have nothing to do with our boundaries, they involve the boundaries of others.

In this way we can see that not only do boundaries define the limits of our legitimate power, they also limit the power of others over us. The responsibility of parents to protect their children cannot be used as a cover-up to repress all sexual information. The responsibility of parents to monitor their children's safety cannot justify their becoming sexually invasive and refusing to allow the child any privacy. Negotiating the boundaries between parents' responsibilities and children's needs is an ongoing, never-ending and subtly nuanced process dependent on the child's maturity.

Boundaries are how we make it possible to explore our sexuality while at the same time trying to make sure that the exploration is reasonably safe for ourselves and others. Reasonably safe does not mean perfectly safe in the sense that sex, like many other important parts of life, is never perfectly safe. Sometimes we get hurt when riding a bicycle or going swimming. Sometimes cherished beliefs become discredited in light of new information. Sometimes our pride becomes wounded when we realize that we may have been thinking in ways that make no sense. In dealing with sexuality, we sometimes get hurt, physically and otherwise. This pain of disappointment or disillusionment is normal and no cause for alarm.

In your need for sexual boundaries, you are perfectly normal. Others may have different boundaries, but all of us need boundaries— not to hide from our sexuality but to make our sexuality safe for us to explore and understand. Your need for sexual boundaries may seem burdensome at times, but as you learn about your sexual boundaries they will keep you safe as you explore your sexual world.

The need for sexual boundaries begins at birth and never goes away. You may not fully know or understand your own need for sexual boundaries, but rest assured you are normal in needing such boundaries.

we're all like this | **STEVEN ING**

chapter 6 | PRIVACY

We all need to be free from the watchful eyes of others as we go about the private business of our lives. Most people seem to understand that whether we are writing a letter, having a personal conversation or grooming ourselves in the bathroom we have the unquestioned right to privacy and others do not have a right to intrude upon this privacy. Generally such a right is not even questioned unless the matter has some sexual component. When talking about sexual matters some people feel they have the right to intrude upon others concerning a number of private sexual matters.

For example, when a child is exploring his own body in a manner that is not harmful or socially inappropriate because the child is doing this exploration in a private place, some people feel a need (and even an obligation!) to inject themselves into the matter because of their own discomfort with the notion of human sexuality. This is a violation of the normal right of any child to privacy and this violation is without any compelling reason, such as the child's physical safety. There is no support for such an invasive act.

Similarly, when consenting adults are alone, there is no compelling reason for anyone to become involved in discovering who is doing what and to whom. This is no one's business except for those adults involved.

Some people try to control others' behavior. This is a serious violation of privacy. But the most excessive violation of privacy comes in the form of those who wish to control not only our behavior but our very thoughts, especially our most personal thoughts, our sexual thoughts. All of us have the right to have private thoughts. We may choose to share them, but that doesn't mean we are required to do so. Our thoughts are our own; they belong to no one else. Healthy individuals know about this need for privacy and will respect your needs. Healthy families respect the sexual privacy of even the youngest and weakest members of the family. Healthy communities have far too many other pressing matters to be concerned with such private matters.

Sexual privacy ensures our freedom from unwanted exposure with its resulting feelings of humiliation and judgment. Our need for sexual privacy begins in our earliest days and is part of our learning about sexual boundaries. In turn, without sexual privacy, there can be no concept of sharing or of intimacy because we have lost the ability to share when we our privacy is invaded.

Your need for sexual privacy is perfectly normal. Others may have different needs for privacy but all of us need privacy in one way or another. Your need for sexual privacy is lifelong and will never go away. Your own need for sexual boundaries may not be fully known or understood by you (or by others) but rest assured you are normal in needing such boundaries. You have a right to insist that others respect those boundaries until you change them. Your need for sexual privacy, like most of your sexuality, will change as you mature and grow.

we're all like this | STEVEN ING

chapter 7 | CONVERSATION

We are a social species; nowhere do we demonstrate this more than in our need to talk to one another. We share ideas, we find them provocative and think about them, eventually discarding those that seem foolish and personalizing those that work. Conversation is the primary way we learn; even books are simply the record of one side of a conversation. No one would argue that we would be better off without talking about the important matters of life, although many have tried to control what they see as a dangerous flow of ideas from one person to another.

This process of learning and becoming wise through conversation is as true of sexual matters as it is of any other human experience. Great countries build universities as places where the flow of ideas can educate and serve their countrymen. Great societies understand that people need to talk about all dimensions of their human experience—including sex.

People need to be free to talk about sex. Allowing an idea to be examined in conversation is the best way to discover the truth about it, saving us from having to learn through painful personal experience. Adults who don't want to talk about their sexuality often learned to repress their need to converse about sex from their own parents, who often learned to do the same from their parents or some other authority.

People are afraid to talk about sex because human sexuality is a powerful force. When others want to control our sexuality, they try to control our thoughts about it by forbidding conversation about sex. They often try to get control by using fear—but mere talking and thinking is not harmful.

We need to talk about sexuality the same way we need to talk about all important things; we need the collective wisdom and experience of the community to help us master and intelligently direct this powerful force for good in our lives.

Talking about sex helps us place sexual matters in perspective. We learn what sex can and can't do for us. For example, we learn that sexual desire and sexual acts can never alone make a bad relationship good. We learn through conversation with friends and family how to talk to our own mates and children about sex.

Practice in talking about sex helps us to learn how to talk in a manner that strikes the balance between frankness and politeness. In some situations, a more vulgar or common vocabulary might be alright (as with some close, same-aged peers) and in other settings a more reserved tone might be called for. With practice, all of us can learn to discuss sexual matters in as frank and straightforward a manner as necessary, no matter what the circumstances.

In your need for sexual conversation you are perfectly normal. Others may have different ideas about what they need to talk about but all of us need conversations about sexuality. Your need for sexual conversation begins shortly after you begin speaking and never goes away. These conversations are not burdensome because they are informative, telling you a great deal about yourself and other people. Others may find such conversation annoying or even shameful, they may even become critical of you for this sort of conversation—but these reactions are about them and their histories. They have nothing to do with you. They may try to silence you through shaming you by invoking some higher authority, spiritual or otherwise. It will help you in such moments to recall that the highest authority, that responsible for reality itself, is also responsible for making all of us into the sexual beings we are.

we're all like this | STEVEN ING

Sexual play and sexual humor refers to the sexual content in funny jokes, amusing stories and entertaining games people of all ages play. Some overly serious people are highly critical of such behavior which they see as vulgar, irreligious or "just inappropriate." They have little tolerance for handling such a serious subject in such a lighthearted manner. But that is precisely the point of why we need sexual humor. We need humor to help us relax and come down to earth a bit.

Sexual humor helps us to approach a very serious and very important subject that would be too intimidating to approach without humor. Humor is the gift that sometimes helps us relax when we are overwhelmed. When we make jokes on any subject we sometimes become tedious and offensive to others. Practicing sexual humor will help us learn to judge our listeners' openness to such humor more accurately over time. With practice we will learn when we can safely make jokes and remain free of criticism.

Sexual play, like the verbal play of most humor, is how children learn about sex. In their sexual play children are trying to understand the differences and similarities of the two genders. In their sexual play they are attempting to learn how to perform sexual behaviors (as in kissing games or conversation games). In their sexual play children are attempting to master important roles in being human, engaging in the reproductive survival of our species.

The need for sexual play begins at a very early age as some infants play with their own bodies and the breasts of their nursing mothers. This need for sexual play never goes away. Children need sexual play to develop normally and learn about their roles and how to interact with others as they get older. These games usually consist of exploratory games and kissing games and should be with peers of about the same age.

Adults need to play for much the same reasons as children as sexual play with their partner is part of adult development and learning how to interact with others. Their play, humor and games with their partner help promote feelings of intimacy, safety and acceptance.

Not knowing about your need for sexual play (or repressing that need because of the disapproval of others) doesn't mean you don't have such a need. Sexual play keeps us from taking ourselves too seriously as we grow older and begin to learn. Your own need for sexual play and humor may not be fully known or understood by you but rest assured you are normal in this need to make and hear jokes, play games and interact with others in a playful way. This play does not mean you are not approaching the subject of sexuality without respect (as some claim). Firemen, lawyers, police, doctors and mental health therapists and soldiers are all doing very serious work. We all are doing very serious work—which is why sometimes we need relief from that seriousness. Far from meaning we don't care, our humor and play allows us to be more caring. Humor and play allow us to be and feel safe when dealing with sexual matters. This safe feeling will give you the power to explore your sexuality and understand this powerful natural force. Although your needs for and tastes in sexual humor and play will change and develop over time this need will never go away. Our recognition and acceptance of this need will help us as we learn how to be more loving sexual beings.

we're all like this | STEVEN ING

chapter 9 | DIGNITY

Our sexuality is the most personal and sometimes, the most private part of who we are. Our need for sexual dignity refers to our craving for acknowledgment and affirmation of and respect for who we are sexually. In the same manner that we need acknowledgment, respect and affirmation for every other dimension of the human experience, we crave respect for our sexuality. Feeling respected imparts a safe feeling. Feeling safe sexually provides us with the courage to explore and learn about our sexuality with the dignity of ambassadors going into a foreign land. The absence of sexual dignity promotes fearfulness and feeling all alone. We do not merely desire such affirmation and the dignity that follows from it; we need this dignity.

Young people often have sexual questions, feelings, thoughts or behaviors. Some uninformed people tease them about such matters. Often, these same people would not believe it right to tease the same young people about their thoughts, their feelings or any other aspect of their being. Teasing children for their interest in sexuality, their thirst for sexual knowledge, about their bodies or their first sexual behaviors is a violation of the dignity of the young.

Sexual dignity is the most important of all our needs because it encompasses all of the others within it, all of our boundaries, our needs for knowledge and our needs for safety—all of them. Without them all there can be no dignity.

Guarding our sexual dignity and that of the people around us (young and old) makes it possible for us to embrace the virtue of truth since it is our fear of ridicule that makes it so hard for us to seek the truth about ourselves and to tell the truth about ourselves. Sexual dignity informs our sexuality with a lifelong knowledge of the right way to be treated and to treat others.

In your need for sexual dignity you are like all other people. You were born with this need and it will never go away. You may make jokes, play games and otherwise playfully enjoy your sexuality, but in all of this behavior there is an essence of dignity derived from knowledge that you are right in being exactly as you are. Some of us learn irrational beliefs or other forms of misinformation about our sexuality; these and other deficits do not entitle others to mock or demean us. The proper response would be conversation about the matter, characterized by an open exploration of what is true and what is truly good. Not knowing about your need for dignity doesn't mean you don't have such a need. The need for sexual dignity may not be known by you or those around you, but nevertheless you need sexual dignity to be able to know yourself and face who you are sexually. Your own need for sexual dignity may not be fully known or understood by you but rest assured you are normal in having this need. Your need for sexual safety will change and develop over time but your need to be respected will be essential to your mental health for the rest of your life. Our recognition and acceptance of this need will help us to live our lives intelligently and successfully.

WHEN WE BECAME OLDER

We are sexual beings from birth and, just as we change and mature so too does our sexuality. In addition to those sexual needs that we acquired in our earlier years there comes a time when our bodies begin to more closely resemble those of the adults around us. Just as our physical and emotional needs change as we mature—so too do our sexual needs change. This time of amazing and wonderful transformation is called puberty.

Our newly acquired needs do not erase the needs we acquired earlier. Our need for sexual dignity, sexual safety and age-appropriate sexual information remain and they too continue to evolve. All of these needs, remember, come under that heading of "that which is required, not to survive, but to thrive." Normal adult development and normal adult life depends on our getting these needs met properly in their time. Starting with the need for sexual thoughts and ending with the need for an integration of our sexuality and spirituality, all of these needs are clearly part of who we are as we sexually mature. Our ability to intelligently manage our sexuality is dependent on our having the words to describe our sexual needs. These words make it possible to share our sexual needs with others in ways that are kind, respectful and helpful to all concerned.

we're all like this | **STEVEN ING**

chapter 10 | THOUGHTS

No one questions the right or need to think...except when we think sexual thoughts. In this one area of the human experience some people are confused and even critical. This confusion and criticism come about only because they are not clear on the facts about human sexuality. There is really no mystery here since we already know that we routinely think about everything within our experience including the most unusual and the most everyday matters. Considering this simple fact it would be laughably naïve to believe that people don't think about sex, that we don't all think about sex.

These thoughts begin at an extremely early age, even before we have the vocabulary to describe matters. As very young people we notice Mommy and Daddy kissing, but they are kissing in a way that is not at all the way they kiss their children. Merely noticing this fact of life is part of our sexual learning and, rather understandably, we wonder about the meaning of it all. As we wonder we try to sort out what feels good and what we like from what we don't like and what makes us feel bad. We are also learning what is right for us and wrong for us.

Some people try to control our thoughts and some even try to control whether we think at all! These "thought police" do more harm than good because life goes much better with, rather than without, thinking—in all matters. Your understanding and the intelligent management of your sexuality is essential to your happiness. Your sexual happiness is dependent upon your thinking clearly about sexuality. Thinking clearly about such sexual matters is a result of lifelong practice in such thinking. Thinking is a practice, not an event.

In your need to think about sexuality you are perfectly normal. Others may have different ideas about what you should think about or whether you even should think about such things at all, but all of us need to think long and hard about such an important part of our lives. Your need for thinking sexual thoughts, once begun, is lifelong and will never go away; such thinking helps us to figure out how to live our lives sanely and happily. Others may find the idea of your thinking about sexuality annoying or otherwise disappointing, they may even become critical of you for this sort of inner dialogue—but their critical behavior has nothing to do with you—it is a reflection on their own discomfort with the subject. They may try to shame you by invoking some higher authority, spiritual or otherwise. They would prefer that you repress such thoughts because they consider them dangerous and out of control...perhaps even a sin. But repressing thinking about sex will only make you less able to manage this powerful human force. Our need to think about sexual matters begins at the early stages of learning and this need never goes away.

we're all like this | **STEVEN ING**

chapter 11 | FANTASY

To engage in fantasy is to dream while awake, allowing us to consider possibilities of all sorts. Sometimes we fantasize about having more money, better health, being stronger or prettier and so on. Sexual fantasy refers to what we are doing when we think about topics that bring us sexual pleasure. We are using our imagination to consider the possibilities of different sexual scenarios. It is a bit like trying on new clothes in a store; we can try them on, just to see what we think, without the expense of actually spending any money. This is what happens with sexual fantasies as we "try them on" to see how they suit us. Everyone does this, no matter what they say.

Fantasizing about our sexuality is wonderful in that we can consider any idea without any downside—without the risk of rejection, getting emotionally or physically hurt, experiencing inconvenience or embarrassment. This is why we have a need to fantasize: we are able to consider many notions in fantasy, but in reality they may simply not work and we would never want to act on all of them. For example, our fantasy may involve illegal behavior that, once we consider the legal consequences, is entirely too costly to us on a personal level. Similarly, our fantasy may simply be too unworkable to ever allow us to have a normal life if we were to pursue it, such as establishing a sexual relationship with a celebrity living on the other side of the world. More common would be having a sexual fantasy about being with someone who, besides being sexually desirable, is unknown to us. Such a fantasy allows us to consider only the sexual dimension of the other person but that person may have other traits, in addition to their sexual appeal, that would ruin any real attempt to have a relationship. For example, we may find out (or we may already know and simply fail to appreciate) that the person is a drug addict, an alcoholic or at the very least, they may have an appallingly low standard of personal hygiene.

Sexual fantasy allows us to experience pleasure—quite a benefit in itself—but sexual fantasy is also the first step in thinking through the consequences of our sexual matters decisions.

Not knowing about your need for sexual fantasy (or repressing that need because of others' disapproval) doesn't mean you don't have such a need. Engaging in sexual fantasy helps us to imagine sexual situations and how pleasant they could be…but is also the first step toward thinking of the consequences of our sexual behaviors. Your own need for sexual fantasy may not be fully known or understood by you but rest assured you are normal in this need to construct sexual stories ranging from the very brief ones to those that are complicated and have lots of details. This way of thinking about sexuality does not mean you are approaching the subject of sexuality without respect (as some claim) but that you need to mentally try out sexual ideas in just as you try out financial fantasies or wonder about what you're going to make for dinner. Far from meaning that we don't care, our fantasizing about sex allows us to be more caring. It is a more serious way to allow us to be safe and feel safe when dealing with sexual matters. This safe feeling will give you the power to explore your sexuality and understand this powerful natural force. Although your needs for and tastes in sexual fantasy will change and develop over time the need to fantasize will never go away. Our recognition and acceptance of this need will help learn how to be more loving and more intelligent in our management of our sexuality.

we're all like this | STEVEN ING

chapter 12 | TOUCH

We know that humans need to be touched and that this need never goes away. From birth, our need to be touched is widely documented and universally accepted. That humans cannot thrive in a life where they are never touched in a loving way comes as no surprise to us; our bodies tell us this every time we savor a hug from a friend or a family member.

There should be no surprise (but there widely is) that as we develop into adults we begin to need to be touched sexually. This need is little understood as we touch ourselves in ways and in places that we never before did. The welcomed touches of others are often not only exciting, but also calming and even nourishing. But, over time, we notice what feels good and, conversely, what fails to feel good when we go too long without being touched by someone with whom we have an intimate relationship. We begin to learn that we cannot by ourselves take care of this need. We are designed for relationship, for community.

Without this touch we become out of sorts and not ourselves. Eventually even others notice this and may make comments to us or to others about noticing that…"it's been a while." In fact we do often become moody, irritable or simply sad after a significant amount of time has passed. How much time? This is a question based upon the individual's needs and no two of us are exactly alike. Some feel an uncomfortable sense of neediness after a relatively brief time and others a relatively longer time, but all of us have a need to be touched in a sexual way and without that touch we begin to behave strangely. Our neediness in this matter can lead to a sense of desperation and a craving to be touched by someone, anyone—sometimes even those we normally would never find attractive. Some people Some people even marry one another out of such neediness alone—never a good idea.

The need for sexual touch begins as we grow toward becoming adult sexual beings and this need never goes away. Many ignore or deny such needs and they are the worse for it. Such individuals are to be pitied as they do not have the skills or perhaps they simply lack the belief system that would allow them to get their needs legitimately met. Not knowing about your need for sexual touch as an older person doesn't mean one does not have such a need. Others can see it in you and truthfully, your own body tells you of this need by how wonderful it feels. Your own individual need for sexual touch may not be fully known or understood by you but rest assured you are normal in your need to be touched and to touch others in a sexual manner. As we get older our need to be touched in this sexual manner, once fulfilled, is not only pleasurable but calming as well—very much like getting any other need met. Although your needs for sexual touch may, and likely will, change and develop over time this need will never go away. Our recognition and acceptance of this need will help us to live our lives honorably and intelligently.

we're all like this | STEVEN ING

chapter 13 | DESIRE

In any discussion of sexuality, topics will overlap. Some might think it strange to need a separate discussion of sexual desire after we have already discussed sexual pleasure and sexual release. But the different words also refer to different important dimensions of sexuality. Sexual intimacy refers to our need to safely share who we are and to know others for who they are. Sexual release refers to our need to obtain relief for sexual tension. The need for sexual desire refers to the need to simply have sexual longing for another.

Some see sexual desire as dangerous. Sometimes they feel this way because their life experience has brought them pain and perhaps some of their pain was connected with the idea of sexual passion. This is a bit like looking suspiciously at books because sometimes people act in destructive ways after reading about an idea—in a book! They conclude that books, after all, must be the culprit because the dangerous behavior occurred after reading a book. This is a bit like blaming cars for teenage pregnancy because the teenagers got pregnant by having sex in a car. The point is that simply because someone did something after having sexual desire does not mean that having sexual desire caused that behavior.

Some people believe sexual desire is dangerous because their religion (or the way their religion has been explained) says it is. But any religious belief that does not correspond with the known truth about our humanity is most likely a misunderstanding of that religion's teachings.

The sort of desire we are talking about here is neither intellectual, nor only emotional, nor simply spiritual. To understand why we need sexual desire in our lives, consider having no desire in any other dimension of the human experience. For example, imagine having no desire for food. Those who suffer from a lack of desire for food, suffer greatly, both physically and mentally. Their physical health fades and all health in their lives goes by the wayside as they decline. In contrast, consider those with a healthy appetite, who approach food with gusto and enjoy themselves: they enjoy life and health.

In a similar way, imagine having no desire for learning or for love—such a person would be stunted in their humanity. Part of caring for someone means wanting them to be able to enjoy normal desires.

Imagine a person devoid of sexual desire. They would have no motivation for marriage, for family, they would have no way of understanding others, including their own spouses and children. No parent, regardless of their personal discomfort with human sexuality, wants their children to be completely lacking sexual desire. To genuinely not experience sexual desire would make one less than human. So we do not merely have sexual desire, we need sexual desire. It is one of our common foundations for a sense of empathy and a motivation for teaching us how to love those so different from ourselves.

The need for sexual desire begins at a relatively young age and shows itself in each of us in a variety of ways. As we get older our need for sexual desire grows. Not knowing about your need for sexual desire doesn't mean you have no such need. Not knowing that your need for sexual desire is universal may cause you to conclude that there is something wrong with you—or with others for having this need. Your own need for sexual desire may not be fully known or understood by you but rest assured you are normal in your need to feel sexual desire and there is nothing wrong with you for feeling this normal human hunger. Recognizing and accepting this need helps us to live our lives with inner peace and intelligence.

we're all like this | STEVEN ING

chapter 14 | TO BE DESIRED

The most universally shared experience of any member of a social species (like humans, monkeys and whales) is the need to feel that one is a part of the group. As we become sexually mature, our need to belong evolves.

For example, what young child can tolerate relentless meanness, abuse and exclusion based upon nothing more than his or her gender? It would be unreasonable to think anyone could tolerate this, much less a child. Nor could any child tolerate even simple passive disregard, cold shouldering and exclusion. Those who treat children in such ways do them great damage.

We all understand without controversy our need to find someone with whom to share ideas and for their reciprocal need to have others share ideas with them. We may not need to share ideas with everyone, but we certainly need someone to do so.

We don't argue at all about the need for people to be desired or wanted emotionally, socially or spiritually. Religions don't argue against this idea—they celebrate it. Governments ask all of their citizens to be involved in public debate. Education systems exist, in part, to make sure that everyone grows up to be a desirable part of a workplace. Only on the subject of sexual desirability is there a hush of ignorance from organized culture.

This hole in our civilization's education of its people is often exploited by those seeking profit in the form of a vulgar commercialism. We see the selling of products to enhance desirability, seedy industries designed to profit from selling the message "You are desired," and "Here's how you can be more desirable," or "Here's a guarantee that you will be desired"—if you get this surgery, use this fragrance, dress this way or make this much money.

Can our needs to be desired change over time? It would be surprising if this were not true, as all of our needs tend to change over time. But it is also true that our fundamental needs do not go away until we die.

Our need to be desired is wonderfully fulfilled when we sense that we are wanted by someone we like. Our hearts soar with joy when the desire is mutual—but we even feel a lift in believing we are in some ways always desirable. The thought that others cringe from the idea of touching us in an amorous way is hurtful to us—and we often cope by reminding ourselves of others who do not pull back from that idea. Fairy tales are full of stories of the meanness shouted by the insecure to the oppressed, "No one will ever want you!" These fairy tales exist as part of our culture's plan to give hope to everyone—that the ugly duckling, the orphaned servant girl, the oppressed slave will all find desire in the future.

Some are afraid of this business of being wanted or desired sexually. The problem is often not that they are feeling desired but the way they think about such a situation. Not unusually, the person who is desired may simply panic because they irrationally believe that the desire of others creates a threat to themselves or brings an obligation that was never there before. These are irrational beliefs.

The need for to be desired is part of our innermost being and develops as we get older. This need never goes away. Not knowing about your need to be desired doesn't mean you have no such need. It simply means you may not be able to manage such a need intelligently. Your own need for sexual desirability may not be fully known or understood by you but rest assured you are normal in this need; everyone has the same need. Acceptance of this need will empower you to have your needs rather than your neediness having you and causing you to behave in regrettable ways. Accepting your need to be sexually desired will give you the power to explore your sexuality and understand this powerful natural force. Although your needs for sexual desirability will change and develop over time this need will never go away.

we're all like this | STEVEN ING

chapter 15 | INTIMACY

To know and to be known is the essence of love and connectedness. We all desire and need to be known by others. We need someone, but not everyone, to know about our thoughts, our feelings and the stories of our lives. This desire is the desire for intimacy, that is, the ability to safely share who we are with others. To be interrogated, as the police question a suspected criminal, is not what we are talking about. Interrogation is not a way of sharing who we are that feels safe. Tearing the truth out of someone is not intimacy—it is the opposite of what we are calling intimacy.

For example, we desire to know others intellectually and knowing others in this way is a pleasure. But the pleasure of knowing and being known intellectually is not merely a pleasure—it is a need. We feel starved when this need to share isn't met. This need may be met by some teachers, friends and parents—but not all teachers, friends and parents. Rarely can one get all needs for intellectual intimacy met with one individual.

In the same manner, we desire others to know us emotionally and we desire to know them and their feelings. To know others and be known is part of what we mean by love. We will be able to safely share more feelings with some people than with others. Others may avoid sharing their feelings with us or find us so controlling in this way that they avoid us altogether. Sometimes the other person is the one with the critical or controlling attitude—and we avoid them. In either case or in the case where both are critical, no intimacy can develop because no safe opportunity to share exists.

So it goes with every dimension of our experience. We are part of a social species and this fact is written into our genetic coding. We do not merely desire to share who we are, we *need* to share who we are. The desire to share who we are is universal. To repress this desire is to repress our need to be fully human; the challenge is finding how to safely share who we are in this sexual area of life.

Every child grows up with a need for safe places where and safe people with whom he can share who he is. As we grow older the need to share who we are in this way becomes more intense. Sharing who we are sexually can take many forms and usually has nothing whatsoever to do with being sexually active. Even the completely sexually inexperienced may have wise older people, spiritual mentors, and good friends with whom he can feel safe to explore his sexuality. Many adult men find that they are able to more safely share who they are sexually with the right group of men than with the very woman whom they love above all others.

We have a natural and healthy need to share our sexual thoughts, feelings and the vast world of our sexuality with someone who is safe and respectful of us as human beings. We want to be known in this way and this need to be known never goes away. Your own need for sexual intimacy may not be fully known or understood by you but rest assured you are normal in your need to be and feel safe when seeking out a way of being known sexually. This safe feeling will give you the power to explore your sexuality and understand this powerful natural force.

Although your need for sexual intimacy will change and develop over time, the need itself will never go away. Our recognition and acceptance of this need will help us to live our lives intelligently and successfully.

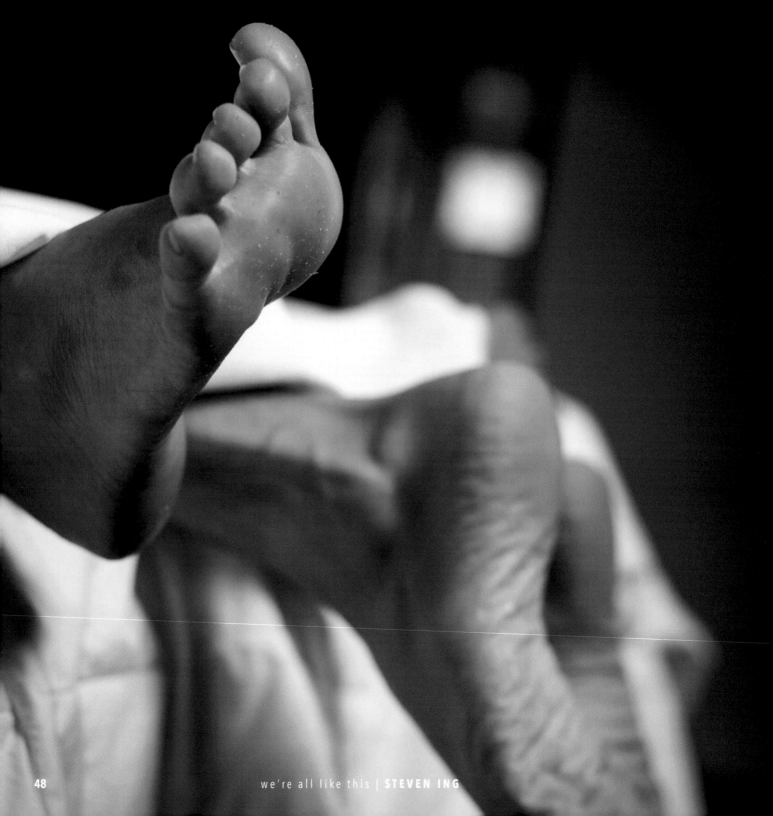

we're all like this | **STEVEN ING**

chapter 16 | PLEASURE

Some might think it strange to discuss our need for sexual pleasure. Others may believe that although we may *like* sexual pleasure and we may *desire* sexual pleasure—nevertheless we don't *need* it. We have dealt with this way of thinking in the Preface, but to restate, we can talk about a person's needs in terms of *surviving* or *thriving*. Parents are thinking of thriving when they talk about how their children *need* an education. Children know they do not *need* to do their homework and they are thinking of surviving.

Many think of sexual release as *the* sexual pleasure; but sexual release refers to a specific need that normally (but not always) involves pleasure. Sexual pleasure is a much broader concept. In the same way that eating is pleasurable, planning menus, shopping, preparing food and serving a meal can also be pleasurable; so too can sexual release be understood as a small part of a larger whole. In this manner, we can see that even the sexually inexperienced may enjoy the pleasure of simply looking at someone attractive or fantasizing about finding someone to love in a romantic, that is, sexual way.

No one dies if deprived of sexual pleasure; one simply becomes less human with the prolonged absence of such pleasure. One fails to thrive—just as with our need for adequate sleep, love or education.

Examples of sexual pleasure include thinking about being in the company of someone you find attractive, or considering the possibility of a first kiss, or merely contemplating going to a public area where you might see (and be seen by) attractive people. These activities provide sexual pleasure; the only reason I am motivated to think about or act on such ideas is to obtain pleasure. These examples remind us that sexuality is all around us. Sexuality is much more than just sex.

No one questions the right or need to experience pleasure—except when discussing sexual pleasure. In this area, some people are confused, critical or frightened because they do not understand sexuality. We give ourselves permission to enjoy physical pleasure in every other way—food, clothes, massage, movement and so on. Considering this simple fact it would be odd to believe that the mere experience of sexual pleasure should be suspect or illicit.

In your need for sexual pleasure you are perfectly normal. Others may have different ideas about what you should think about or whether you should experience this sort of pleasure, but all of us are designed to respond to pleasure in an affirming way. Why would we be made this way if merely experiencing sexual pleasure (whether through thought or physical experience) was wrong? Your need for sexual pleasure, once begun, is lifelong and will never go away—even if you live to be old and frail, your fondest sexual memories will always please. Others may find the idea of your thinking sexually pleasurable thoughts or engaging in sexually pleasurable behavior annoying or otherwise disappointing—they may even be critical of you on this matter. Their critical behavior has nothing to do with you—it is a reflection on their own discomfort. They may try to shame you by invoking a higher authority, spiritual or otherwise. They would prefer that you refrain from such pleasure because they consider it out of control and therefore dangerous. Some even consider any sexual pleasure to be automatically a sin. But repressing all sexual pleasure will only make you less able to manage, guide and direct this powerful human desire in legal and honorable ways. Our need to experience sexual pleasure begins at a very early stage of our lives and this need never goes away.

chapter 17 | RELEASE

Everyone needs to relax from time to time. As youngsters we may feel anxiety about some sort of performance such as homework or a piano recital, wondering what others will think of us and whether we will do a good job. We feel tension when our parents argue. Resolving the tension (after the recital, finishing the homework, seeing our parents make up) is a relief and we feel better.

But when young people start getting a bit older they begin to experience a sort of tension that is different from any they've experienced before. Their bodies are becoming adult and they start feeling adult sexual feelings. Sexual tension is one of those feelings.

Sexual tension can take some time to finally arrive in our lives or it can seem to appear overnight, but the simple presence of sexual tension is normal; it is part of being alive and fully human. Sexual tension is like the hunger for food: we all experience it regularly, and we all have different levels of hunger, some of us eating more and others less.

Sexual tension eventually is resolved through sexual release. Whether we call it sexual release, climax, orgasm or some other term is unimportant. The feeling is, at first, like satisfying a hunger we didn't know we had.

How to achieve sexual release is a matter of some controversy. Certain cultures or subcultures have different rules than others. Some families have their own messages about what is and isn't appropriate. Even some individuals within a couple have differing ideas. Some individuals even use religion (and a great deal of energy) to direct others in the manner that they have been taught is the right way to deal with sexual tension. In all of these families, cultures and religions, the issue is how to achieve sexual release honorably and legally. In other words, we all have to meet our sexual need for release in ways that observe our society's rules (that is, legally) and our own personal, internal rules (that is, honorably). Yet some who are in positions of authority over us are extremely uncomfortable and even ignorant about sexual matters. For such uninformed people even the idea of a need for sexual release is repugnant and to be avoided in conversation. Occasionally, such people set up rules so that there is no honorable or legal way of obtaining sexual release; this is inhuman since no one can control the mere presence of such cravings. Not teaching people how to honorably and legally obtain sexual relief is also inhumane in that the failure to do so is cruel and abusive.

Certainly the most universal and acceptable manner of obtaining sexual relief is to engage in the self-stimulating, self-gratifying practice called masturbation. Virtually everyone on earth does this at some point; those who say they don't (or never have) are generally lying.

Sometimes people consider marriage to be the only manner in which one could acceptably fulfill this need. As good as this idea may be, we must remember that it should be discussed at length by the two people considering marriage, as no two people have synchronized schedules of sexual needs. This discussion seldom happens in many communities because people are often not taught how to talk about such matters. In these communities great unhappiness and marital failure can result from simple and preventable sexual incompatibility. In the best of situations, all couples learn to care for one another despite their differences in this matter.

The need for sexual release begins as we get older and it never goes away. You may not fully know or understand your own need for sexual release, but rest assured you are normal in your need for and in your efforts to obtain sexual release. Accepting your need for sexual release will empower you to have this need rather than your need having you. Managing this need will give you the calm to consider your sexual choices thoughtfully and powerfully.

we're all like this | STEVEN ING

chapter 18 | IDENTITY

Solving the problems of life is the central drama of survival but, if we are fortunate, our problems evolve beyond mere survival. As we master the more elementary needs of food, shelter and safety we eventually run into the *rather delightful problem* of *how to be happy*. This problem is difficult to solve. Many times, we simply fail to understand ourselves and what we need; sometimes we don't know who we are. An example of this would be a man who takes a job solely because his father wants him to rather than because he wants to. Another example would be marrying simply because others wanted us to do so.

To know *what* one wants is impossible without knowing *who* one is. This knowledge is only learned as a process, not an event. No one can really announce who you are, though they may try. Understanding your identity is a process of discovery over time, through experience. We learn through trial and error—through our mistakes. No one gets these things right the first time. I thought I would like the clothes my friends liked…until I discovered my own sense of style. I thought I liked the most popular music…until I discovered my real preference. I thought I wanted to be something I knew about until I took a class in something I knew nothing about.

This process is true of our sexual identity, as well. We are always learning who we are because we are always growing and changing. We used to hate eating this food, now we love it. We used to think kissing was an awful, ridiculous idea and then, little by little, we changed. Some of us even grow to like kissing.

But if I'm always changing, what is my true identity? The answer to this question goes to the core of who we are and that core never changes. Our personality is the same whether we become factory workers or physicians, whether we think we are one way sexually— and then discover we are someone altogether different. Our sexual identity may best be understood as the latest incarnation in our development.

We don't argue that workers have a right to be workers, that writers have a right to simply be who they are, that friendly or unfriendly people have a right to be who they are or that very intelligent or less intelligent people have a right to be who they are. Social, political and even spiritual preferences are generally, even if grudgingly, accepted. Only in sexuality is this matter of identity controversial—in some places to the point of social shunning, incarceration, or even death. But, no matter how difficult it is, we are as stuck with the need for a sexual identity as we are stuck with ourselves. Without knowing our sexual identity, it would be impossible to gauge compatibility or embark on long term relationships with confidence and dignity. For example, not knowing about how much you like kissing could lead you to marry someone who doesn't like kissing at all. That would never work.

Our needs for sexual identity include requiring respect for our real sexual selves, allowing ourselves simply to be ourselves, and giving ourselves the permission to discover who we really are.

This is not to say that we will not make mistakes in understanding ourselves. Some of these mistakes will seem immediately funny, other mistakes will take time to understand, still more serious mistakes may require deep forgiveness from ourselves and others.

Not seeking our sexual identity at all or failing to accept our identity would be failing to accept life as it truly is. No one else can fully inform you who you are. Accepting your identity and especially the darker side of that identity, the side you don't show just everyone, gives you a sense of solid ground beneath your feet.

The need for sexual identity begins at birth and never goes away. You may not fully know or understand your need for a sexual identity but rest assured you are normal in this need to be uniquely yourself in sexual matters. Knowing your sexual identity will fill you with power to make informed choices in your quest for happiness. Your sexual identity will change and develop over time. Recognizing and accepting this need will help you live intelligently and successfully.

chapter 19 | ACCEPTANCE

Only the most sickly among us need to be accepted by everyone. Yet there remains the truth that ours is a social species and that we all need acceptance by some in order to feel comfortable. Although many have survived without acceptance by others, none have thrived for any appreciable length of time.

So we exist within a balance of independently going our own way with integrity and not bowing down to the herd, but in that same ruggedness needing connection and affiliation with others. The more intimate parts of myself are shared with fewer and therefore, I need fewer people to accept these parts of myself. But the fact remains that, to be healthy, I need someone to accept me for who I am sexually. I need people with whom I can safely share the intimate parts of myself. My failure to find these accepting people propels me toward depression and I will experience a shortened and more miserable life.

Most people have no trouble accepting these thoughts, even if reading these ideas for the first time. Most all of us accept that one's more intimate feelings should be shared only with one's more intimate friends. Likewise, we accept that one's more intimate thoughts need to be shared with those who are able to accept us even after hearing our wildest, most creative thoughts. Few, however, have articulated the absolute need for humans to find those with whom we can safely share our sexuality and still remain connected by this intimate bond. We need to accept one another because we need to be accepted; there can be no community without this mutual acceptance.

Examples of our failure as a species to accept others sexually are many. Some of us have made fun of youngsters' natural ignorance in order to get them to stop asking sexual questions. Some of us shame those who do not agree with our sexual beliefs. Some of us have criticized people for exploring their own bodies or their own sexuality in even the most benign ways.

Sometimes we romanticize this need and rely on finding a romantic partner who can accept me as I am and love me as I am. But our need to be accepted is far more vast than any one person could take care of. I must somehow struggle to find a space for myself in my society if I am to feel comfortable, safe and at peace.

Withholding the acceptance we need is a sort of violence done to a member of a social species by the community. We forcibly hold this individual apart from us when they so much want to belong. Will the need for acceptance change over time? Some of our needs, including our immature need to have everyone's acceptance will hopefully evolve—but the need for some acceptance is still there.

The need for sexual acceptance begins at birth and it never goes away. It includes acceptance of our gender, our sexual questions, our sexual development into puberty, our sexual interests and so forth. Not knowing about our need for sexual acceptance doesn't mean one has no such need. Your own need for sexual acceptance may not be fully known or understood by you but rest assured you are normal in your need to be and feel accepted when dealing with sexual matters. This feeling of acceptance will give you the calm you need to consider your sexual choices thoughtfully and powerfully. Although your needs for sexual acceptance will change and develop over time, this need will never go away.

we're all like this | **STEVEN ING**

chapter 20 | APPROVAL

Sexual approval is different from other sexual needs. Our need for sexual approval seems…more subtle. Sexual approval is different from desire because those around us can approve of us without desiring us. Sexual approval is different from mere acceptance because acceptance is merely neutral. Our desire for sexual approval goes to the heart of human shame. If our bodies, in their nakedness and their sexuality, were unacceptable then at some core level we are unacceptable. If our social circle withholds approval of our sexual being then we are not part of that circle.

Some worry that, if we approve of others, we become complicit in every sexual decision that they make and for every sexual behavior they engage in. This is not a rational conclusion any more than approving of an anorexic's need for food means we are complicit in their decision to starve themselves. Our shaming of others (as opposed to approving of their sexuality) results in secret-keeping. In the case of the anorexic this can be fatal; in the case of keeping sexual secrets this always results in a breakdown in the ability to intelligently manage sexuality—generally with miserable results.

Our need for sexual approval is akin to our need for sexual acceptance but it is a more intimate need. When we feel safe enough to let others close to us we disclose more of ourselves to them. These people become privy to our more intimate desires, thoughts, fantasies and behaviors. Their disapproval shames us, disinclines us to share further and eventually isolates us if we are not careful to escape such shaming people. Loving people have no such shaming effect. The paradox is that the less control others try to exercise over me the more control I give them…because I love them in return and there is no defense against such unconditional love.

Our need for sexual approval changes over time, as we mature and become more emotionally independent. As a child I may need to be approved of in my gender: that I am a boy or a girl. As an older child I begin to learn about the need for approval of my curiosity—that my questioning is encouraged by my caregivers. As we grow older and experience the sexual wonder and pleasure of first love, that first love also needs approval. Discussing boyfriends and girlfriends is essential to understanding relationships and preparing for successful lifelong commitments—these discussions need to be met with approval. The sexually healthy adult must be approved of in his concern for pleasure. As adults begin to understand that sexual pleasure is far more complex than merely a pleasant touch, they come to understand their broadening need for approval.

The need for sexual approval begins at birth and it never goes away. Not knowing about your need for sexual approval as a child doesn't mean there is no such need. Our needs have always surpassed our understanding of them. Your own need for sexual approval may not be fully known or understood by you but rest assured you are normal in your need to be approved of in sexual matters. The calm feeling that comes from being around approving people will give you the power to intelligently explore your sexuality, to understand this natural force, and this calm will empower you to make better choices in matters of sexual health. Although your need for sexual approval will change and develop over time, this need will never go away. Our recognition and acceptance of this need will help us to live our lives with insight and kindness.

we're all like this | STEVEN ING

Throughout history, as our societies have become more complex and demanding, our need for guidance and coaching has grown. This is true of our careers, social skills, even our complex and demanding new forms of recreation. Not long ago the notion that we would benefit from someone guiding us into healthier eating would have been laughable—no one would have understood why on earth one might write whole books on the topic. Now, no one really questions this aspect of human experience—except in the area of sexual relationships.

While we have many people out there advising us how to "spice things up" sexually, we have others trying to persuade us to "bring it down a notch." These people all seem to feel as though titillation, the arousal to physical sensations, is what sexuality is all about. No one appears to be coaching or guiding the young, the middle-aged or the elderly on how to express their sexual needs in age-appropriate, legal ways. What passes for "guidance" is usually only an elaborate sell-job on repressing sexual thoughts and feelings.

Even the most gifted achievers in any endeavor benefit from mentoring, guidance and coaching. We accept this in sports, where the most gifted athletes receive coaching. We accept this in business, where mentors make all the difference in countless careers. There is no significant field where guidance and coaching is not provided—except in normal human sexuality.

Our efforts at sex education fall short, as they are often an education in anatomy, sexually transmitted diseases, and how pregnancy occurs. This would be like reducing driver's education to car wrecks and auto mechanics rather than teaching people how to drive safely and enjoyably. Our efforts at sex education, if mirrored in cooking classes, would be limited to food chemistry and prevention of food poisoning.

The reason we don't have good coaching in sexuality is that we've never defined our sexual needs. The controversy stirred up by public health officials when they argue for expanding sex education demonstrates that we have no consensus on sexual needs. Once we agree as a society that our children have a need then the argument becomes how to best serve that need. This is called consensus. We usually don't even discuss human sexuality from the viewpoint of needs. The lack of consideration of sexual needs across the lifespan makes it impossible to intelligently discuss a sexual curriculum for youngsters. We need to reach consensus about those needs as a group, and then we will need teachers, mentors, guidance counselors and coaches to assist in meeting this need, just as in every other field of human learning.

Our needs for guidance and coaching change over time. This does not mean that we will necessarily reach a point where we won't need guidance. Our need for sexual guidance include dealing with changes across the lifespan because our goals and needs change as we age. A child needs to grow up knowing where he can go to find real answers to life's problems. Adults have the same need.

The need for sexual guidance begins at a young age and never goes away. Ignorance of your need for guidance hardly means you have no such need. Your own need for sexual guidance may not be fully known or understood by you but rest assured you are normal in your need to receive counsel and guidance in sexual matters. The confidence you get from knowing will more than offset your lack of experience as you discover, explore, and grow to understand your sexuality.

we're all like this | **STEVEN ING**

chapter 22 | SEXUAL RISK & ADVENTURE

There is no learning without stepping into the unknown. This feels risky and adventurous. Stepping into the unknown is essential to a healthy sexuality because we change throughout our lives. For example, some individuals who were never comfortable with hugging may one day come to understand that they need hugs; others who never wanted to talk about sexual matters may one day surprise us with penetrating questions or comments. Just as people change in every other dimension of life, we all change in the area of sexual thoughts, preferences, and fantasies. Adventuring into the risky unknown is an essential part of sexuality.

We were designed for learning and adventure; a lack of adventure and exploration leads to boredom, which can lead to foolish risk-taking just to relieve the tedium. Our need for taking risks is often repressed or shamed by others because they blame risk-taking for the destruction of families through affairs and divorce. But risk-taking within relationships actually promotes long-term stability by developing intimacy.

Some people misunderstand their own need for sexual adventure as a purely physical need, and they look for different sexual experiences of a physical nature to satisfy them. This will never work since human sexuality is a larger, vastly more far-reaching concept than mere physicality.

Some of us mistake sex itself for intimacy. Intimacy is the ability to safely share myself with another. To confuse sex with intimacy is like confusing a bite of food with the larger notion of nutritious cuisine. Couples who cannot find a way to safely share themselves with their partners will find that no amount of sex can satisfy their loneliness. For them, at best, sex serves to distract them from their aloneness. Such people often become preoccupied with altering the more superficial aspects of their sexuality, changing the locations for sex, the clothing one or the other will wear, and even perhaps changing partners in the hope that they will find something satisfying *on a purely physical level.*

There is nothing wrong with doing any of this. What is wrong is to think such changes *are* the adventure when they are but a small part of it. Many people who appear sexually adventurous have never taken the chance of letting someone know who they really are—their feelings, their goals, their fantasies, their histories and so forth.

It would be far more frightening and hence risk-taking to begin really looking at who we are and thus risk self-condemnation. The next step would be letting safe people in our lives know who we are and thus risk disapproval and even humiliation. Finally, letting our partners know who we are risks rejection and abandonment. This is risk-taking on a grander scale. A wild sex life is not about how many positions you can get into or how often you have sex—wildness is a result of facing our fears.

Our need for sexual adventure changes over time. We may need to explore different aspects of our sexuality, find a partner more willing to take the journey into the darker waters of the unknown—but the need is still there. Satisfying our deepest sexual needs leads to the risk-taking of disclosure, which always helps others know us better. And after getting to know you better, let's face it, others may not like you or want to be around you.

The need for sexual risk-taking and adventure begins with our first furtive attempts to find out what it's all about, like our first kiss. This need never goes away. You may not fully understand your own need for sexual adventure and risk-taking but you are normal in your need to take sexual risks. Understanding this need will help you manage your sexual behaviors, including your disclosures, with wisdom and foresight.

we're all like this | **STEVEN ING**

As we get older, develop the need for a type of love that is not satisfied by the hug of a friend are a relative. There are many forms of love, the love of a mother for her child, the deep love of friends and, as we get older, there is a need in everyone for the type of love that can only be given by someone who loves us in a sexual manner.

But do we need such love or are we simply indulging lust? Many people who mean well teach that we do not need sexual love, we only think we do. They teach that those who pursue sexual love in a manner that goes beyond what they consider acceptable are consumed with lust or in the parlance of modernity, "behaving inappropriately." Some parents teach about sex in this way. They do so because they have seen the destruction caused to one's life in the pursuit of sexual love. Such parents and other adults have mistaken the poorly thought out search for sexual love (with the scandal, the law breaking, the unwanted pregnancies and so on) with the need itself. This is a bit like confusing our need for transportation with the poor results of train derailments, plane crashes and arrests for driving while intoxicated and then denying the need rather than working to improve the odds of our success.

When a feeling of neediness is universal and thwarting such a need results in a failure to thrive, then we can know with confidence that we are dealing with a human need. To call this need something else, especially something evil or vile, is only a reflection of a lifelong discomfort with one's own sexuality. Attempts to repress the need for sexual love have been not only unsuccessful but have often brought about the very results that were most feared.

When we provide those around us with no honorable and legal means for them to meet their needs they are condemned to meet those needs in some way that is dishonorable and illegal. But no one is at fault for having a need universally held by every member of their species. Those of us who are responsible for teaching the children of our society—parents, teachers, religious leaders, all of us really—have often failed to teach young people how to get these needs met legitimately.

When we are older people, our failure to meet our need for sexual love often results in impulsive acting out. Such love-starved people find themselves behaving in ways they normally never would. They sometimes hurt themselves and others through secretive affairs or sexually criminal behavior. More often they cause tremendous, but more banal problems by making commitments to people with whom they should never have gotten involved.

Can our need for sexual love change over time? Some parts of this need (frequency, quality and manner of expression) may evolve—but the need will always be there. The need for sexual love begins in our older years after childhood and this need never goes away. Not knowing about your need for sexual love doesn't mean you have no such need. Often, sometimes to their amusement, others can see this need in us before we do. Your own need for sexual love may not be fully known or understood by you but rest assured you are normal in your need to feel sexually loved and to share your love with someone else. The wonderfully powerful and transporting feelings that attend fulfilling this need will help you to see the world in a more loving and forgiving way. Although your needs for sexual love will change and develop over time, this need will never go away. Our recognition and acceptance of this need will help us to live our lives joyfully, intelligently and successfully.

we're all like this | STEVEN ING

Integrating our sexuality with our spirituality refers to our need to allow the sexual part of us to talk to that part of us that seeks meaning in the world. Allowing my spirituality to be informed by my sexuality keeps me from becoming out of touch with the truth about who I am. My spirituality provides my sexuality with meaning, context and depth and, by doing so, can explain my sexuality, preventing it from becoming shallow, and even worse, boring. Indeed, sexuality and spirituality each become boring without the other.

Some believe we can only be spiritual through organized religion, but we know that humans existed as spiritual beings long before the development of religion. Religion can be part of spirituality but doesn't have to be the only expression of spirituality. Many people have very strong beliefs without being religious. Examples of these beliefs would include thoughts about the nature and purpose of our existence, the role and importance of love, and one's own personal reason for living. Spirituality is never closed off to the anti-religious, the agnostic or the atheist—everyone is spiritual.

Without being informed by our spirituality, our sexual lives would be permanently cut off from intimacy, love, and family. Attaching meaning to sexual activity informs us of all of the other needs discussed in this book. We would know nothing of our sexual need for safety, for example, if we didn't value human beings. Valuing humans is part of our spirituality, held in common by all spiritual teachings.

Some forms of spirituality are anti-sexual. They are also anti-human. They attempt either to place inhumane controls on what is normal or to throw off all restraints and deny the spirit's need for safety and honor. Both extremes fail to allow these parts of who we are to exist together. One example of anti-sexual spirituality is the kind that fails to inform us how we can meet our sexual needs in a realistic, honorable and legal manner. Such spirituality often attempts to deny human needs. Any form of moral teaching that fails to consider sexual needs leads to suffering and is neither spiritual nor moral. The other extreme is spirituality that attempts to deny meaning to sexuality and throws off all care for others. This approach fails to show us the beauty that is beyond words and reduces sex to so much less than it really is.

Both these forms of spirituality are anti-sexual because they fail to teach about the beauty of sexuality. They are anti-human because they deny the wonder of sexuality. The first is too controlling; the second, too thoughtless.

Most often people seem to put sexuality into one part of their mind where they keep their sexual feelings, thoughts and behaviors. They have another part of their mind set apart for spiritual matters. The two parts never seem to talk things over. People who live like this do not allow their spirituality to inform their sexuality or their sexuality to inform their spirituality. When people who live like this get into an organized religion, their religion may be socially approved, but it is not kind, loving or genuinely forgiving. If we cannot love and forgive this most intimate and fundamental part of our experience then it makes no sense to talk of mercy. Others with a failed integration of sexuality and spirituality may develop a faith that is strict—but not strong. Generally, such faith focuses on rules but fails to incorporate the eternal principles that attracted people to it in the first place.

The need for integrating sexuality with spirituality begins at a young age, grows more intense as we mature and never goes away. You may not fully know or understand your own need for integrating sexuality and spirituality, but rest assured you are normal in having this need. A deeper spiritual awareness will give you the power to more deeply enjoy your sexuality. Confronting your spirituality with your sexual needs will help your spirituality become increasingly down to earth and help you evaluate the spiritual words of others. Your spirituality will become more real and more human as it deals with sexuality. As you integrate these aspects of yourself, your sexuality will become more meaningful and your spirituality more illuminating.

IN PARTING

It may sound like scientific heresy to say it but we don't need studies to demonstrate that we have sexual needs. Our own bodies tell us; this truth about ourselves lies within. Here's how you can prove it for yourself by performing a series of simple thought experiments for each of the chapters in this book. Simply imagine having the perfect life with every conceivable need met in a full manner. This would include the perfect relationship and the perfect sex life. Then, in the context of all this perfection, all this bliss, consider the consequences of subtracting any one of the subjects in the chapter headings. A perfect life, perfect relationship and perfect sex life...but without any humor or play: is it still perfect for you? Is such a humorless, serious as death sort of sexuality still perfect? Is it even sustainable? What about sexual intimacy? Sexual approval? Sexual information? For the vast majority of humans the answer would be a negative one. Such a life is not perfect, nor is it sustainable. There are those who live such lives and they may be surviving but they are definitely not thriving.

This book represents a beginning. The words above offer a beginning view of human sexuality in a truly human context. But despite every effort to present these ideas in an inoffensive manner that would be truly helpful to all there will doubtless be some who are very offended by any real discussion of human sexuality.

This is quite understandable. Human sexuality is frightening in the same sense that anything unknown and strange is frightening. Also, just talking about any taboo subject is frightening to many of us who have never been taught any way of talking about these things.

But there is another fear that is a bit less human than it is institutional. For most of recorded human history our species has lived a life separated from the truth our bodies would have instantly revealed. The fundamental idea of this book is that we have sexual needs and that those needs are not sexual desires. Yes, we have desires but that truth does not negate that our desires are mostly based on our needs.

The notion that there are sexual needs brings with it a major institutional problem: the problem of control. Specifically, the view of sexual needs shared in these pages threatens those institutions invested in controlling people in our political, social and religious spheres of influence. The controlling of humanity cannot be better achieved than by utterly controlling humanity's sexuality. But controlling people in this way is only possible if one gives up the notion of sexual needs. Once this notion is accepted then each individual has a right to get those needs met and every system that pretends to serve us (our governments, our religions and our social institutions) must allow us some legitimate and honorable way to get our needs met.

For example, the religion that is more fixated on maintaining its brand purity than in the safety of its own children will often flex its power to extinguish discussion of any failing in this area—which makes the danger escalate. Any government that aspires to serve its people but fails to provide equal opportunity and protection because of gender or sexual orientation is failing to meet the sexual needs of its citizens. These failings are often excused on the grounds that religion demands, say, a different standard of rights for men and for women or a different standard for the heterosexual majority than for the others.

Our needs are different from mere desires. They have a legitimacy that mere desires cannot claim. Because of this reasoning, any self-serving institution that exists by controlling human sexuality will find this book threatening. But there is no institution that must of necessity find this book threatening. If our understanding evolves then our institutions can evolve as well. This they must do if they are to truly serve us. To the degree that our institutions fail to serve us they exist only to control us. Thus they lose their legitimacy and our loyalty.

None of this is to say we must live in a chaotic society without law where every crazy person gets to act out on every impulse. But our laws, our rules and even our beliefs must make their peace with our humanity and our very human sexuality. This will take some time. The time that it takes will be too long for many but we must begin somewhere. So let us begin a conversation that has been delayed long enough.

we're all like this | **STEVEN ING**

SEXUAL BILL OF RIGHTS

Human beings have the right to have their needs met. It is morally wrong to deprive children of education or anyone of food or medical care and so forth. In the same way, people have sexual rights and they include:

The right to be a sexual being; to feel sexual feelings, think sexual thoughts and engage in sexual fantasy and consensual sexual behaviors and conversation, including the right to privacy.

1. *The right to a personal sense of humor and playfulness about sex.*

2. *The right to sexual information that is appropriate to my age and needs.*

3. *The right to be accepted and protected as a sexual being, with my gender, thoughts and preferences, by my family, my mate and my community.*

4. *The right to an education that integrates my sexuality with my beliefs without that spirituality being turned into a tool for repression of normal human sexuality.*

5. *The right to protection from unwanted sexual attention, words and acts directed at an individual.*

6. *The right to read material with sexual content.*

7. *The right to evaluate potential mates for sexual compatibility.*

8. *The right to change my thoughts about any aspect of my sexuality without being punished.*

AFTERWORD

I am unaware of any systematic proposal of the sort of thinking found in this book. This book's core notion is that we as individuals have sexual needs that are pervasive, enduring and central to our core notions of what it means to be human. I have no doubt that once the idea is widely accepted, its self-evident truth will have historians of the future finding it quite strange that their ancestors ever labored under such ignorance.

The notion that people even have sexual needs will seem incendiary to some even as they admit that the most innocent of babies has a need for sexual safety and that even the youngest of school children need role models. The acceptance of such needs is likely to create an awareness of the need to reorganize much of human society. This new awareness will likely be very disconcerting to some. This is true because we are only able to justify ignoring such needs by denying they exist. Admitting these needs exist would require our governments, education systems, prisons and the justice system, relationships and even religion to give in a bit if the notion of human sexual needs achieved widespread acceptance.

The entire basis for the thought that we have sexual needs is grounded in my experience but is confirmed by an argument confounding to some: that is, that we as human beings have no choice about what we need because we simply need what we need—there is no choice involved. This thought removes the force from the arguments flowing out of divine revelation (of whatever origin). If there were widespread acceptance of the central notion that sexual needs existed entirely independently of the will, no religion could then employ the shame and condemnation common to past centuries to control whole populations. What shame could there be for simply being human? The notion of sexual needs, even the term itself, undercuts the notions of moral ignorance common to many forms of spirituality.

Once the notion of sexual needs became widespread, the notion of sexual rights follows. From that notion there would be pressure on all human institutions and relationships to allow for this otherwise obscure dimension of the human experience. For this writer that more humane, more human future cannot come quickly enough. If we accept the notion that there are human sexual needs, then we must provide for a human way, an honorable way, a legal and legitimate way for all of us to get those needs met.

ACKNOWLEDGMENTS

Any book of this sort owes its existence to many individuals who participate in its making. This writer feels a deep sense of gratitude to the many who served as visual models for the ideas expressed in words. Without them and their playful participation these ideas would seem far less human. Their courage is highlighted by the fact that many who were asked to consider modeling for the photos in this book were far too intimidated by the subject matter to get involved.

Our photographer, Chris Holloman, deserves special recognition for his professionalism, artistry and his humanity in telling the pictorial history of human sexuality in a manner that depicted human sexuality in a human context. He and the models made this part of our project have the safe look that eases the growing global conversation away from fears of either repression or of vulgarity. Human sexuality never looked more beautiful.

The entire team at Sexual Futurist supported this project from day one with their ideas, emotional support and practical help—all of which served to affirm the necessity of this project's existence. Thank you John, Michael, Nicole, John, Jesse and Valentine.

Surprising to some is the vital role my work with sex offenders has played in creating this book. Countless thought experiments with them where we asked the question, "If you had everything else going for you in a future relationship but you didn't have x, could you be happy?" Without sexual safety, sexual knowledge, sexual humor, play, spirituality? Each man and woman's answer to this question was another inspiration for this book. These individuals, who can do nothing to change the past, have shown extraordinary courage in their close examination of the past and their willingness to learn from it and to eventually transcend it. Their collective wish is that others might learn from their mistakes and thereby avoid them.

This writer is no exception to the fact that all married authors have an obligation to acknowledge their spouse's role in the creation of their work. In this case, my wife Sharon served as art director for the photography sessions and primary editor of the words of the text. But far more than that, living with her for the last 20 years has allowed me to experience what it's like to have every sexual need met in the fullest manner possible. The wonder of knowing her has been transformational and the words on the pages here reflect the reality of our life together.

Lastly, this writer acknowledges the countless sexual futurists around this planet of ours who want to be free (and who want others to be free) to look at human sexuality from the perspective of reason and knowledge. This includes those sexual futurists who love their religion and who know that their faith has nothing to fear from humanity sexuality. Bless those who look forward to the deeper understanding of their faith aided by this perspective of the truth revealed by their own bodies. This author can imagine those brave grandparents who place this book on their coffee tables for their grandchildren to look through during a visit. Or those mothers who read aloud to their children from the most tender years, reading a page or two here and there to inform their children not only of the information on the page but to free their children to think rationally and talk openly about sexuality from the perspective of human dignity. Fathers who read this work for themselves and their children will enjoy "having the talk" far more than they ever could have believed possible.

Questionnaire: Are My Child's Sexual Needs Being Met?

Many people will find even the asking of this question to be challenging if not offensive. But for those thoughtful parents who are open to the ideas expressed in this book, the question is easy to imagine facing in a straightforward manner. All child have physical, emotional, and intellectual needs and we have no problem considering these--why not face our child's needs for sexual safety and age-appropriate sexual information in the same way? In order to help families find a reasonable way to assess their treatment of their child's sexual development the following statements are offered. A range of numbers (from one to five) follows each of these statements; one indicates "poorly" and five indicates "superior." Obviously an answer like "five" indicates it's time for a pat on the parental back just as a lesser answer indicates there's room for improvement.

1. When asking their immediate caregivers questions about the human body and sexual activities, my child feels safe and is safe from inappropriate shame or ridicule.

1   2   3   4   5

2. My child is protected from information that would be above and beyond their ability to process in an emotionally comfortable manner.

1   2   3   4   5

3. My child is allowed access to age appropriate information that satisfies their curiosity and prepares them for the next stage of learning.

1   2   3   4   5

4. My child is not shamed, ridiculed, or exploited for expressing thoughts about sexuality, feelings that are sexual or behaviors that do no harm to others.

1   2   3   4   5

5. My child's statements of discomfort with how they are treated in sexual matters are taken seriously and respectfully and I make sure of this.

1   2   3   4   5

6. My child has been informed regarding his need of and right to privacy so that he can begin to observe the privacy needs of others.

1   2   3   4   5

7. My child is allowed and encouraged to talk about and otherwise intellectually ponder human sexuality.

1   2   3   4   5

8. When it comes to sexuality, my child is allowed to laugh, make jokes and engage in age-appropriate sexual play with peers and safe adults such as parents.

1   2   3   4   5

9. My child may get mocked about sexual matters because no one can be protected at all times from all people, but to the degree that a parent can, I have guarded my child's sexual dignity, including remarks about their body, their questions, their play and so forth.

1   2   3   4   5

Questionnaire: Are My Sexual Needs Being Met?

When in a relationship, my partner may have a difficult time listening to me talk about my unmet sexual needs without taking my comments personally. The following questionnaire is truly about the individual, not the relationship. The questionnaire is based on the notion that, as an adult, I differ from a child in that I personally am responsible for seeing to it that my needs are met. This questionnaire is meant to be taken both by those in a relationship and those adults who are not in a relationship. My needs, after all, are my responsibility. If I do have a partner, I am not absolved of my responsibility to care for myself. A good place to begin taking this questionnaire is to start by taking the one for children, while thinking of my own childhood. This will help prepare the mind for seeing more than otherwise might be discernible.

1. I give myself permission to simply have my sexual thoughts rather than repressing them. I encourage myself to think deeply about what I am thinking and how I came to think that way.

1   2   3   4   5

2. I acknowledge to myself at least that I engage in sexual fantasy and that being aware of my sexual fantasies is a normal part of intelligent management of my sexuality.

1   2   3   4   5

3. I know that, as an adult, I have a need for sexual touch. I may not be getting that need met but I have my need instead of my need having me.

1   2   3   4   5

4. I love sexual pleasure and am comfortable with loving it.

1   2   3   4   5

5. I understand that the need for sexual release (orgasm) is normal and that, whether single or in a relationship, I need to take care of this matter.

1   2   3   4   5

6. I need to feel safe to simply be the sexual being I am and, if in a relationship, I have negotiated my way to getting this need met.

1   2   3   4   5

7. I know I have a need to be desired and I have built a life that enables me to proceed mindfully and

intentionally.

$$1 \quad 2 \quad 3 \quad 4 \quad 5$$

8. I enjoy my sexual desires. They are a vital part of a healthy sexuality; nevertheless, I have evolved to the point that I have my sexual desires rather than their having me.

$$1 \quad 2 \quad 3 \quad 4 \quad 5$$

9. My sexual identity is an important facet of my life. I am who and what I am and I like myself.

$$1 \quad 2 \quad 3 \quad 4 \quad 5$$

10. I have intentionally pruned away those who cannot accept me for who I am and I have just as intentionally surrounded myself with those who can accept me.

$$1 \quad 2 \quad 3 \quad 4 \quad 5$$

11. Those who are a part of my inner circle offer me the same level of approval that I give myself; I do not have to fake being someone different in order to achieve an illusion of approval.

$$1 \quad 2 \quad 3 \quad 4 \quad 5$$

12. I surround myself with those people, books and influences that help further my sexual development and understanding.

$$1 \quad 2 \quad 3 \quad 4 \quad 5$$

13. I allow myself adventure; I even pursue it in a manner consonant with who I really am and who I want to be. I take appropriate risks in a manner pleasing to myself.

$$1 \quad 2 \quad 3 \quad 4 \quad 5$$

14. I am intentional about integrating my sexuality into my romantic pursuits, especially in my primary relationship. I am assertive about pursuing sexual happiness.

$$1 \quad 2 \quad 3 \quad 4 \quad 5$$

15. Sexually speaking, I am less concerned about rules than about the more important guiding principles of my personal spiritual path. My spirituality provides context and meaning to my sexuality and my sexuality grounds my spirituality in a helpful way. I have found an honorable way to be me.

$$1 \quad 2 \quad 3 \quad 4 \quad 5$$

CPSIA information can be obtained at www.ICGtesting.com
Printed in the USA
BVIW12n2354050216
435315BV00019B/110